HART ISLAND

HART ISLAND STACY SZYMASZEK

NIGHTBOAT BOOKS

NEW YORK

Hart Island is an island in New York City at the western end of Long Island Sound. The island has been used as a tuberculosis sanatorium, boys' reformatory, and an asylum. It is currently the location of a 101-acre potter's field, which is the largest tax-funded cemetery in the world. More than 850,000 bodies are buried there. Despite being tax-funded, public access is severely limited and controlled by the Department of Correction, whose inmates from Rikers Island are tasked with conducting the burials. This means that people who know or suspect they may have a loved one buried there cannot freely (if at all) visit them.

The literal place in this poem was my day-to-day life between 2008 and 2010: my routes through the East Village, my job (at The Poetry Project at St. Mark's Church, which is the site of a cemetery where civilians can visit the graves of New York notables like Petrus Stuyvesant and Daniel Tompkins), things I heard and overheard, and my sense of history (defined by Charles Olson as "the *function* of any one of us"). Hart Island is both Manhattan's, and also, this poem's, shadowy unconscious.

A sense of purchase guides the human bone.

Dale Smith

Just put me on Second Avenue; I can hang on.

Paul Blackburn

‡

a cavern hill-

side hazel

eye carnation

face nasal call

a drake

messianic chemical

reaction scourge

marks of the lot

lit infra-

red winding

paper napkin

Turin

‡

scout in December when

DNA is a frozen box

of letters a poorly

insulated mid-life

apartment empty

condo views bake

a pie to test

the oven drape

moves extra-

mundane

‡

the F

Financial advisor

by itinerant limbs

I mean free of circulation

plods and plots I lie

rate of interest

in disease is not hypo-

condria hypo-

thyroid feet

are cold plugs

grip portfolio

expound line

item no 401(k)

no ponzi

‡

woman applied

for disinterment Hart

Island chaperone leads

her to "he calleth his

own by name"

manifest with a

number she chews

the mouth has to

go dry a rose

a day a congenital

day

‡

small pine

grid crown sky-

line this form where

I feel love

for babies

Catholic and "regular"

then SC-B1 1985

first AIDS baby

buried deeper

than yellow fever

‡

the polity

around visitation

through Rikers

inmates inter

dead matter

"easy duty"

brought back

to community

‡

the avenue

downtown

quality of leg

pain predictor

of blood clot

church clock still

broke

will work for poets

‡

beware there is nothing

to fear! scan of

thorax indicates

possession the dog

buries her treasure

in meatspace

‡

insolvent

malfeasant

debate in summer

08 it costs more

than a penny

to mint a penny

now activated

charcoal stomachs

‡

Madonna and child

a citrus offering

a captain's cross

fresh trench anchored

by mussel shells

no exhumation record

of the bodies beneath

the Waldorf Astoria

‡

citizens freeze

on the avenue

film crew warms

in a row of trucks

a church

lives off artists

frozen citizens

arrive with numbers

in trucks

‡

Crane agora

frosted eyes lift

altars along the Eastern

Seaboard and Melville's

in the Bronx

parts of Dawn

Powell science

didn't use

her executrix

refused

the field claims

     ‡

coffee and kasha

coffee light and kasha

with gravy or borscht

hot or cold smiles

at me everyone

who works here

on the avenue

‡

the other is another

literal body oh limit

and radiance we breath

the heated mousy dust

in the church

love nest

‡

island of near

million unvisited

named for its organ

shape defunct

missile silo lunatic

shoe compost TB

limb box Academy

Award winner un-

identified in East Village

tenement dividend

to start again

soft body area

by 25 years

‡

Long Island

Sound salaried

ferryman

drive combat space

graft of shrub

upon my face spit

feathers

‡

the window evinces

the boarded

window figure-

head looks away

from his marker

feels unfriendly to change

my regular order

when the guys

say "coffee and kasha!"

and smile like that

‡

eye spasm

in the field

unpublished female

camaraderie Russian

baths oak leaf de-tenser

better than beating self up

over a roll of posters fight

for greater storage

index card era putrid

sprouted onions in mesh deity

donation station enough

scrap copper to

start wire mill

‡

photographic evidence

circa late 20th c.

shows clock at 6:20

being right twice

a day isn't so bad

follow confidant into steeple pass

through whale ribs to

see park from air rights

‡

one million exhausted bodies touch

totally compos mentis ex-missile flue

empathy of cold terror air

conducts brainwaves where the wardens

prohibited themselves

‡

railroad appliance extraction

code violation sub rosa hovel

trunk of party favors but places

are only as large as our largest organ

‡

can I stay to ride

the 2nd Ave. subway?

ultra-low-sulfur bus

no schedule advertisements

for shoes disturbed walk

around manholes and

grates poor electrocuted

and fallen friend eggs all

in one basket "the calming

effect of contact"

‡

I think I would like to remember
any day of my life like
super-autobiographical memory
people remember every day
of their lives a video quality "I go on
scraping the potatoes" narrating
the kind of lover I would be in
a rent controlled apartment

‡

archivist on the end of expired
tap from-below POV
in shopping for history
books my Romanov name-
sake murdered on my birth-
day a leafy branch grows
from my forehead and

like an idiot I weed it

the value of an extra orifice

in secret RIM society

‡

pre carpal tunnel peri sciatica post

varicose potbelly bath business

enter editor in eight

fields in eucalyptus room

full story on the damage

of a poet

‡

Koch built work camp

quality of life exiles 1982

send-a-message bodies

F hangs out beneath

the river nothing across

the PA system is so

cuts to service so broken

windows theory so zero

tolerance rhythm of our

geese and vegetable offer

lays waste to anti-circadian

intrigue slump of my shoulder

below attitude of her

head in prayer

‡

11:44am became spring

snow New York City news is New

Jersey news so why this ambulance

again who knows these histrionics

about snow in spring how long

how long before our bodies

can merge with air

‡

overshoot notary

caught in other fantasy

"you again" the one who forgets

to sign in the presence of

Carmine so many frozen

yogurt spaceships landing

next to banks

‡

proper amount of space

between bodies changes our

heavy weights form a sightline

for frenetic birds you don't

need to know someone's name

why we need sexual activity

prohibited signs suffer the morning

in royal blue robes

‡

half way to Brooklyn dawns

on me debut of new female

voice doomsday budget so

worth $2.50 lull of mechanic

female voice waxes on and on

the job a fabled nurse

backward to Coney Island

my own wracked trillion

messages of pain

‡

rephrase line about muskets

and takeover for facilities

question bodies grow titan roots

on an island fish head souls

plaster the head of a train no

we do not malinger we stop

for breath on the island

for sale eat packing peanuts

move small archive on high

for typhoon Mary's

                     high tide

‡

sent this poem to friend

in prison wardens confiscate

for cryptic word games possible

porn faulty padlock during

anti- suicide sweep confiscate

Lennon shirt "New York" a

series of locked boxes

‡

Holy Saturday physical

rest before distribution

of milligrams outcasts

are exemplary Christians

in a system of civic

palindrome as in god

saw I was a dog and

didn't disjoin me

aspersed the meat

in my basket

‡

to live rearguard within

our means to live

non-bloodline to live

in arbitrary mealtime to

accept the island as a

regulatory function "the 'black

spot' where the no-go

zones meet flesh"

‡

"These New York
City pigeons are not
calm" they think I am
a saint when they form
an air shaft that forwards
me through the park
to the church

‡

put tie and rose
on for party see guy
with *Tottering State*
many familiar
faces but friends
in far hoods hands
take the brunt of all
of my falls a friend to

Band-Aid brand resolve

to be a better body

of knowledge a creature

with bolts bred out

but a big hugger

‡

disambiguate state

of linen risen

or materialized an oxic

extra-organ for spring

break ocean-of mercy-

side imbibers whereas

these wounds fasten

to each other

economy-sized keloid

formers without pressure

garment obsessive mantles over

shoulders of land

‡

hold finger in

glass of salt

water try

to empty of its

Eastertide relationship

to infection

is early return

to island via charter

where in Paramus

moon is dying camp fire

a catch cooked in foil

where in Egg Harbor

my threshold was higher

‡

Mohawk flanks another day

at the ranch if not for

the roses proffered rapier-like

wouldn't recall frontier

romance enter old ironsides

true south skewed

from the grid make way

around assembly at lion

for tour of ghostly friends

      ‡

cross avenue to preempt

green awning market employee's

song a crush unrequited

made PSA trust at 50%-

off-sushi level tangency stands

in for intimacy appeals

to pals once you see the

body hurling out its broken

chairs congress of vital

undead hunters laminated

blood chips chalk it

up to biological event

‡

this typewriter obsidian

mausoleum stuffed with cherry tiperillos

"OH

FERNANDO

WHY"

‡

viewfinder City

Island just a citizen

nyc.gov Shred Fest be

first with your personal

docs for a free shredder

Brinks truck for identity

treaties covenants leases

pitch for oblivion

oak's obituary

half-ton of victory

parade confetti

where is he? we are

standing on him

‡

ghost bike for fallen

unknown riders pigeons'

iron beaks navigate magnetic

beam of chopper light all

out on balconies with crank

radios my friend diazepam

too many citizen arrests

"ignite the timber of your

public promise" sell a shallot

that rolled into liquid garbage

door another rider the pigeons

lock beaks in the foreground

‡

try to establish habits in the West

ancient grains and someone more

objective to mess with "often

die in garrets" bookkeeper

says these jobs are mangles open

your processionals discovery of Static

Guard as flammable altar girl "is

dancing on dynamite" HR/BP

acceleration in canine

absentia familial tone shock

after science makes gay rat

saturate chest with

prescription oxygen

‡

fix broken safety

culture like NASA

thinking foam don't

hurt swill live sour

kraut bloody

mary mix

ban emails in

and out of this room

‡

"involve body in muscle

memory" hit mailbox and

pharmacy veer away from

HRC kids who see easy fix

for marriage money no

grail collects the blood

via undressed living

space flush dirt from poor

tile job poorly tiled face

enter the yard where

everybody knows the sexton

is the saint

‡

monument to the un-

befriended built by

the imprisoned *Peter Pan*

to *Dirt* Oceanside CA

cenotaph virtual find-a-grave

flowers from animated

Wendys "custodial staff"

screened for adaptation

to the open

        of open air

‡

disorderly rosebush iron

enclosure undercover mathematics

of growth + Matta-Clark's entropy kids

playing in sand above stone

room you can't excerpt

the island's fat storage officer

says plan an author dinner at

marker no. 95 shove an orange

segment down neck mix with steak

in 6% metal cargoes stumble into

vigilante admin vs. goth gang dry hump

this bell tolled for nobody here but

that nest is made of human hair

‡

the schist the stud/stuff

of the island Jane Q.

Public wistful super-continental

smile in a handcrafted barrel

that screech when pods

encounter a human gelatin drifts

through space to replace

adrenaline mist of merchant

prince body ransom captain

kicked cur dog off

clayey marks portico flag

whipped up stench returned

remains not identified but rigged

with local legend and

device tripping bells

‡

poetry records reveal

women when young

their higher pitch look forward

to stiff silver hirsutism parallax

sleeping pallets throw coins in

ducts and wait for chatter from

weird family first socialist

lesson earwigging with

mother as girls

‡

rush from dark office door
to door consider the "ghost
proposals" tantrum prone peg
leg article 3 remove word
"forcibly" feel card shuffle
in the gin fizz of a lay picnic at least
one of us should be able to fly
with this swab of avian cells
swoop to warm ground schist
sparkle release a homing coo

‡

engineered baritone squeak
foretells we will speak to the
mouse other poets discover
how to get out of the city
not venerate tiny skulls

in summer St. Francis on his

deathbed thanked his donkey

telephone effect warps landline

call turns blessing of the pets

ceremony into pet cemetery

figure cost of living

raises fall on own

sword on a feast day

‡

elaborate sty in my eye

bisection of okra garden

is euphemism for flea

market necropolis so

if I lose you in the street

if I lose you in the street

below par drainage thumbs up

to lotus leaves don't be sad it's

pro it's prophylactic body

pooled with cellulose chewing

up a toothpick

‡

they sleep at his feet

where they would be misty

weather and dust meld

denim into skin

yellow high tops they

sit on him incubate

contact with cellular

device hawking Kewpies

was innocuous before

the chipped slate darling

draws the fangs of philanthropy

they don't read eye-level

words where the eyes would

be where the signs are

eclipsed where the roses

snapped the twine

‡

kid needs to grow into
his feet wants to be the last
American playboy will
still touch the arm of his
sidekick the psychic got new gold
trim economical extraction from
twilight customers WE BUY your
broken chains get two bruised
pears from new all-night cart
cable access pop-in this pineapple
filled with vodka is also very
good for Fire Island

‡

best star sighting director
of neighborhood vampire
flick the horror of being
alone with a paramour who sleeps

with an open left eye the avenue

is lined with Craft Service

giant flat screen of hands

making sushi opt to eat

with the men served by Polish

women in peasant shirts very few

who knew you in the 80s can

bring themselves to know you

now watch

the three-legged rescues

get their evening walks

‡

mid-June Wednesday un-deposited

paycheck dropped calls cop! click

and I'm going into the mountain

errrrr good omen puppy runs

from tattoo shop into avenue and

does not die its humans form

a running mob around it hand

automatic over mouth onlookers

hands over mouth not to die

that way the mnemonic martini

glass shape scar on the thigh

nothing to do

          nobody to see

‡

someone left the bolt

unlocked but he played

midnight sentinel with his

book I closed my eyes

and dozens of poets were

unable to speak this sapling

restores an aura

of dignity down here

there is possibility dead wood

isn't dead figures swim

together my claws don't rush

to fill you for a second fall

in love with the light

‡

you'll eat bread till you return

to the ground fingerless

gloves fingertips around hot paper

cup you doubters you steam flows

from the theater of my ribs

where I dragged a compass

to retrace my area an army

of those who survived themselves

define ecstasy as breath

tinged with a story how I would

offer it to anyone tonight

‡

recused in hallway just happen-

stance a man just expects to find

warmth in a church he'll search

for her in five hospitals follow

her epileptic path extended mass

of her body let's degrade the space

between us the alcohol gets

inside a space heater in Siberia

mesh becomes exposed just

one part piled on another

     ‡

how a body becomes unwanted

yet everywhere touched

buried in married memories

index starting with ear how an ear

becomes unwanted and wears

that indignation whereas a hand

hides its information how a hand

becomes unwanted and works a hoe

with steady pulse it is unwanted

the cargo of bodies cross

             Long Island Sound

     ‡

who's under who's wing

make a pantomime of loss someone made Aspiration a new

arm from sticks and paper

mache he's holding a bouquet

so furtive this is flip phone to flip

phone only a white whale

away here is my card I am not

working is what I will say

here is my card I am not working

today wish friends would re-

populate as quickly as the fields

‡

non-conflict with annual

Day of the Dead home-

coming women with soft

brushes clean birthday

on famed stone not an "active

crack" restricted to its two

halves extension cords hang

from pear branch that is how
water is boiled for food so many
people's people extend into brass
smoke break in shade bodies
spaced by workers

"...is the earth as full

as life was full, of them?"

‡

become one who gets infections
of the ear how to glow during perfect
sorrow storm cotton wick in flirt with
the cries of "muscular
naked babies" muffled then
understand the value of your crowned
organ not effective to use fire
in the hypothetical when
it has already burned

‡

walk up avenue with memory

circling regime query the poly-

clinic supposed to be very old

but that is effect of *maalstroom*

felt as a douche on the mood

of a divided city one can adjust

to anything a child's filled teeth timed

to destruct post-coverage a pile of

lime not calm of a site where a thing

was settled but flooded with hinged

creatures "too much information"

shuns a history of abjection

when she said we don't want

to bleed you but I myself was bled

‡

this veneer of civilization is

"[I have other skills?]" only recently

de rigueur for poets best not say

"[There are other workers]" you

work here sore groin stand-in

for black eye triggered

impulse for some cake you're a big

lesbian wipe off your knees save cry

into wilderness for after dinner

‡

you can't re-

generate a creeping

dose do not touch

me noli me tangere

vigil face set

deep and de-

familiar wonder

what his pen-

ultimate noun

was life here

same old

eat a bag

of seeds

 he liked

 ‡

every point accessible

to your intervention

after snow a new path

reveals harebrained

desire line anatomical

contrabass becomes feeling

when felt at every

point on the avenue

bars too full for numbing

the face of candor

attempt to withhold alas

a question edge closer to

the bells the recording

of church bells

‡

after long engagement with

antisocial dart about as sparks

through stubble when obvious

he is history scent of pine

surrounding drugstore a story

problem with subjunctive math

laugh of the day arrest? I need

arrest "fountain would be

closer" than damaged bath

card an ordeal to relax with

true feelings of commune blinking

lights at Sing Sing the princess

of darkness has a rub out style

food smells from kitchen prepared

containers for disappearance

note from my anatomy we won't

forget how livable you were

‡

variable length session the

thousand and one nights

of therapy a "protracted night

of storytelling" buys time

for the flock for a time such as

this when pissing on graves

isn't an expression look out

the rose window at low budget

sleaze or remember the brink

of an open air piano bar

rumor of a favorite

slave in vault another report

is auditory 99 bottles of rum

on the wall then punchbowl down

an inch the volition to become

a fleck of drywall

‡

1:32pm became

spring in the Eastern

Hemisphere none

of my look backs

look back cell searches

for nearest tower cobbler

makes shoes new some

people burn socks

by 1987 the kid died

a thousand deaths a cover-

up countenance for

running the meeting

                into the ground

‡

sanctuary stripped bare cyclical

illness smoked out in Jamaica

Plain lain upon a pallet hid

too long from the people

those hollows beg for

bodies eat sardine stubs multiplied

into every kitchen one where she

presses the crushed linen

suit repeats March

came and went like a lion

‡

accept postcard for new

enterprise in the doomed space

and presto! wilted red

peppers points to a front

pill box doesn't induce dosage

habit deficient in nearly all vitamins

radical birth structure

reasons winning power

of the chronically fatigued

all starring as Paula in

Gaslight we never took alleged

watch this watch is wound

by the motion of our arm

flipping through script with

underdeveloped denouement

two women in black walk on

opposite sides of the avenue

‡

crocodile tears for the unnamed

dead lures the press what is death

without a ditch what is life

without a sudden pillow dreamed

that all attributes once held

in our hands were gnawed off

by our own fangs we all

smiled into each other's eyes

the patron for orchards the patron

for running water we all prayed

to you for passage to Avignon

‡

first stranger to ever

buy me a drink the charm

of looking disheveled

and looking at whiskey

my bags have bags my one job

gangs up on my other job

worker hoists a giant letter "B"

to the base of a fire

escape today is brought

to us by a lit acronym "life

has its sub rosa hell" a centuries

old expansion plan reps

siphoning energy from where

poems are made a cave of unscented

nostalgia combusts pick the hole

in the wall where you'll never see

anyone you know those misanthropes

you promised to love

‡

"work 24 hour a day shifts" leads not

to the good life will wash once

a day reliquary arm with window

to the past crow perches on

child she drops message wipes

out will wash twice a day

woman denied clearance for

closure use "the state of our

health our teeth our tongue"

read refrain what an archive

is male unknown iron

mouthfeel will wash

three times a day stripped from

the source how long till you

are on your way with

your clean case history

$$\ddagger$$

the roses weren't in the lion's mouth

then they were people line-up for

food enough ego here to lend

to each psychotic candles lit

inside seedy side of serving

broke into a sweat at dhal

cart late spring rain walk on

wet stones a crop of shellfish

can't be afraid of pigeons or

punks the beer can wasn't in the lion's

mouth then it was if I lived here

I'd be home dirty undershirt

and flowerpot even though

"I hate the village"

‡

to fill the space around ID

with lipstick and comb disrupt

third antiseptic shower "hi" that is to say

thanks for my penmanship I don't

pray my narrative had to stop

in 1987 just a little dog to ask

after "we're okay" you couldn't cut

the grass are in a kitchen I can't

picture to fill the space around midnight

stabs at shared medical history thanks

for night owl nature sleep

on a strip of mattress eat

beets out of a jar

‡

communicate real crisis vs.

imagined crisis to the gang

already in raft more Kafka

less Hasek "you think you're better

than a priest?" celebrate Fiscal

Year-Tomorrow popping fuses

still no fiduciary relationship to

disclose old-fashioned with

mottled cherries and cigarillo put

out on branch darling I'd rather

lie down with you than stand

with you more BS less

earthy press for weak spots

out shoots golden ticket you

can leave as corpse or half

corpse after volunteers attack

neighbor's wisteria

‡

trip to notary .99 cent soap and tooth-

paste more expensive pills for exertion

headaches trip on new bike lane

paint cyclists still wowing

lingering over vowels in tandem

with English flutist downside

of beards they get funky

in this heat look for an out who dream

of farming sheep factor break-up of

the camps wish to pinpoint stressed

trees too many dogs in the box

a lighter canopy where they

sat when they talked seeks nothing

in common when conversation

fails there is the mouth so hot

it's borscht on the rocks

‡

forgot to take pill today stopped

taking other pill idiom of

mothering is heavy metal

ballad roll the dice on clot
issue to kill the ambiance down-
ward dog in new context
after last night need a botanical
given epithet leader of the jurors
make it state flower scented

‡

overhear that's a smile
I like lady in green perk
for a day of anatomical
tragedy sit on cement
ledge marshal evidence
of extant routine overhear
she never orders to stay cinephile
suggests more than fondness
for close-ups at 40 got the face
I deserved learn to walk on
busy sidewalk dialog with

likenesses raise eyebrows at

plate of crisp bacon arm

in dirty sling pretend

M15 is a tour bus

‡

places of death redacted

though each unique as in

corner of Broadway and

Houston word like "something"

stands in for what possesses by-passers

to laugh mystery everyone is

reading plot ready as weather

slow to process this shade of

blue about the mouth unique

as in if under an overpass a single

person is missing further

excluded from the heart

of the city no one has the right

to say the world is empty

‡

palpate mature scars going

over handlebars when I had music

and shoes of suede as mute

testament take F to ocean

all sympathy stationed on

a sheet dark vessels lit by ground

show this is your life a flip

book romance tapered into

a night what is known about

October you will dress up

as a famous missing person

‡

this park a space

for symptoms everyone

awkward at goodnight but hold

me close and I'll suppress sound

of breaking bottles die summer

die fit of army surplus tan

hands hold encounters with

ancillary clues our cognitive

problem resolved by repeat music

chipped cartilage floated in

joint space connects to future

motor style out-toeing where

street becomes avenue

‡

big toes taped in new shoes

spy commuter high tops of

hallucinatory therapist sun will set

at 7:10pm elbow taped from bar

table friction post bad date wear

on soles disclose abnormal gait he

thinks shoes and watches are beautiful

storefront praise poem eliminates

dialog around transactions just

put it on the counter weekend

sun will set at 7pm over row

of upended dominos thud

in chest pass bench

make dedication

                upon a golden cannon

    ‡

eat less and from a tin

floss caught between two

fillings observe obsession

feel new hair long in your valley

of death kick the can dress

in white aid of a chantey take

this head-shaped onion

and replicate in wax "layered

in notebooks" the healing

hospital is located beneath

the sick one meet at boiler

first day it fires the feast day

of Cosmas and Damian

‡

take pill on full

stomach polish milk

out of boots when I grow

up it won't be pretty

intensity restored

in analysis hide from

our families behind plexi deposit

documentary mass in short

bios clove smiles on oranges

pomegranate halves with glitter

and stars "because we were

fastened only approximately"

and parochially the fiddler

emerges from the trees too young

to have really been in that war

‡

make fun of to-do list "get pot"
"soak beans" imagine a New Year's
Eve without hot water bottle
pocket *Mrs. Dalloway* search
for own gold lion head cuff
links with ruby eyes anthro-
pomorphize into another cat fight
for the most cloaks deduct flowers
from petty cash look into dirty
kiosk for proper names wait
on bench 1,642 aroused
by bloodshot eyes say the poets
will keep guard over us
who live with our bodies

‡

omitted from survey
of alternative space this

place teaches to endure
skull cup is hidden
in the composition
writers booksellers
secondhand clothes
dealers held at heart
level contains stout
poured from a leather
purse verbal agreement
to sanctify morphs into leech
necklace newly established lock
box in case of need to parse
it out three cultural
neanderthals with night terrors
under the rain spout

‡

Day of the Dead crowned
sugar skulls promiscuously melt
in living mouth typed list

threw it out stand upon

a Dutchman under blue tarp

if I hug you any closer I'll be

behind you funnier today than

when I crushed your tamales

the horror of being conjoined

and losing your weight in sister

calls for split screen effects

heroine afraid of being stabbed

or crushed by falling a/c sirens

down the avenue so often

                      we clasp our ears

     ‡

can mimic pigeon

since fever where it said

you'll be okay not a New

Yorker till a pigeon talks

where they're not supposed

to be see a pair of hawks

Crane's apartment on Pineapple

view now blocked soft spot

for men from Ohio box of

violets settle on your chest

seasonal flu breaks year

into smoky panels

‡

reference card table and

chairs to confusion first pull

of beer watching dimes pile up

can't get a game going lead

with forelock grime mixed

with bay rum and rose you grow

till you get hit then always

trying to form a pack get

a game going shuffle like

the old Poles taught you

‡

psychological commitment of

that test result I fail

the mission shred the wrists

of unhappiness replace fat

with surplus spun wool

footage safe in cold storage

can't see own hump

but will play hunch-

back or crow pluto till the

law of sanctuary is vetoed

neck open to sky with

smooth board slide down

railing at sundown to sexton

interring cluster of ash

make passing valediction

‡

winter brings forth chronic

issues smoke when you

don't smoke what you eat

when alone winter

brings forth bolster

pillow and monographs

studio-sized pine mounted

on pine search of arts patrons

equals list of obituaries we pace

balcony gargantuan folksy

lions I don't know

why do you come here?

one night the gates were left

open and the people who were

sleeping continued to sleep

All quotes in *hart island* were heard (or misheard) and written down in my notebook during readings that occurred at The Poetry Project at St. Mark's Church.

"[poets] work 24 hour a day shifts," a line attributed to Bob Kaufman, was said by Will Alexander on 4 November 2009.

"the calming effect of contact" was said by Keith Waldrop on 18 February 2009.

"I go on scraping the potatoes" was said by Robert Kelly on 18 March 2009.

"the 'black spot' where the no-go zones meets flesh" was said by David Buuck on 30 March 2009.

"these New York City pigeons are not calm" was said by Jayne Cortez on 25 March 2009.

"Oh Fernando Why," (an alternate version to "Oh Fernanda Why"), is an Arthur Russell song and was performed by Arthur's Landing on 6 May 2009.

"ignite the timber of your public promise" was said by Kristin Palm on 4 May 2009.

"[poets] often die in garrets" was said by Samuel R. Delany at the panel on Jack Spicer on 15 May 2009. Delany also referred to Hart Crane's comment about writing poetry as "dancing on dynamite."

"involve body in muscle memory" was said by Carolee Schneemann on 18 May 2009.

"ghost proposals" is from Steve Carey's "Stagerlee" and was said by Anselm Berrigan on 3 June 2009.

"...is the earth as full as life was full, of them?" is a Frank O'Hara line said by Robert Glück on 28 October 2009.

"[I have other skills?/There are other workers]" was said by Catherine Wagner on 21 October 2009.

"fountain would be closer" is from Leland Hickman's "rhapsody Macaulay not historian his story" and was said by Marjorie Welish on 13 January 2010.

"protracted night of storytelling" was said by Jalal Toufic on 3 February 2010.

"the state of our health our teeth our tongue" was said by Steve Evans on 15 March 2010.

"I hate the village" is a line by James Schuyler and was said by Anne Waldman on 21 April 2010.

"life has its sub rosa hell" was said by Alice Notley on 28 April 2010.

"You think you're better than a priest?" was said by Michael Lally on 12 May 2010.

"muscular naked babes" was said by David Meltzer on 26 September 2010.

"layered in notebooks" was said by Laura Moriarty on 29 September 2010.

"because we were fastened only approximately" was said by Ben Estes on 18 October 2010.

p. 7: "Frosted eyes there were that lifted altars" – from Hart Crane's "At Melville's Tomb."

p. 29: "earth / debris / & schist, the stud/stuff of the island" – Paul Blackburn

p. 30: "If I lose you in the street / if I lose you in the street ..." – lyrics from "The Leanover" by Life Without Buildings

p. 33: The 1982 vampire film *Habit* was directed by Larry Fessenden and was shot in the East Village.

p. 35: *Peter Pan* child star Bobby Driscoll is buried on Hart Island. Driscoll was found in an abandoned tenement building in the East Village in 1968. *Dirt* is Piero Heliczer's film that Bobby Driscoll appeared in.

p. 39: "my eyes burn and claws rush to fill them / but in the morning after the night / I fall in love with the light" – line from Psychic TV's "The Orchids"

p. 42: "Aspiration" is the name of one of the statues "which depict Native American men" in the entrance of St. Mark's Church made by Solon Borglum. The other is named "Inspiration."

p. 44: "This land is not the sweet home that it looks, / Nor its peace the historical calm of a site / Where something was settled once and for all:" – from W.H. Auden's "In Praise of Limestone."

p. 54: "When the water / rises, the stones in the piazza / seem to be a crop of shellfish" from Tim Dlugos's poem "The Lions of St. Mark's."

p. 64: "The martyrs will keep guard over us, who live with our bodies, and they will take us into their care when we have forsaken our bodies." – Maximus of Turin

PUBLICATION CREDITS AND THANKS

Sections of *hart island* were published in VOLT, *Peaches and Bats*, *Vlak*, *Hotel*, *Elective Affinities*, and OMG. Thank you to Edmund Berrigan, Alex Abelson, Gillian Conoley, Todd Melicker, Carlos Soto-Román, and Brandon Brown for their support of this work. Thank you to Jess Mynes who published 3 sections as an *Asterisk* folio and to Chuck Stebelton and Woodland Pattern who published 2 sections as a broadside. Deep gratitude to Brian Teare who first published sections from *hart island* as a limited edition chapbook for Albion Books. Thank you to erica kaufman for her support during the years this poem was being written, as well as Brenda Coultas, Jamie Townsend, and Kathleen Miller for consistent encouragement.

For those who are interested in learning more about Hart Island, there is a nonprofit called the Hart Island Project (hartisland.net), headed by Melinda Hunt, that advocates for visibility and accessibility, and maintains a database listing over 60,000 burials. The book *Hart Island* by Hunt with photographs by Joel Sternfeld (Scalo, 1998) is also an excellent resource that helped me envision what is so hard to imagine.

ISBN: 978-1-937658-34-2

Design and typesetting by HR Hegnauer
Text set in Goudy Old Style

Cover and flap photos by Stacy Szymaszek

Cataloging-in-publication data is available from the Library
of Congress

Distributed by University Press of New England
One Court Street
Lebanon, NH 03766
www.upne.com

Nightboat Books
New York
www.nightboat.org

ABOUT NIGHTBOAT BOOKS

Nightboat Books, a nonprofit organization, seeks to develop audiences for writers whose work resists convention and transcends boundaries. We publish books rich with poignancy, intelligence, and risk. Please visit nightboat.org to learn more about us and how you can support our future publications.

The following individuals have supported the publication of this book. We thank them for their generosity and commitment to the mission of Nightboat Books:

Elizabeth Motika
Benjamin Taylor

In addition, this book has been made possible, in part, by grants from the National Endowment for the Arts and the New York State Council on the Arts Literature Program.